THE CABINET OF
THE PRESIDENT OF THE UNITED STATES

The CABINET of
THE PRESIDENT OF
THE UNITED STATES

JAMES A. EICHNER

Illustrated by Tomie de Paola

Franklin Watts, Inc.
575 Lexington Avenue
New York, New York 10022

To Dor and Wadey

CONTENTS

THE CABINET OF
THE PRESIDENT OF THE UNITED STATES

THE PRESIDENT NEEDS HELPERS

FROM THE earliest days of civilization, no leader has ruled completely alone. The simplest tribe has had some kind of council to provide advice to the chief, and even the most despotic government has included, formally or informally, a group of advisers to assist the top man.

Obviously, a man with as difficult and as complicated a job as being President of the United States needs trusted assistants who can carry part of the burden of administering the work of the government, and who can give him advice on policy. One group of top assistants which meets regularly with the President is called the Cabinet. Its members are the heads of the executive departments of the federal government.

Therefore, a member of the Cabinet of the United States has two jobs. He is a trusted adviser who, in theory at least, is available for advice and recommendations covering the whole field of government activity. He is also a business-type executive who runs an organization consisting of thousands of people, not only in Washington but spread throughout the nation and the world. Each job is a demanding one.

Although the duties and the authority for each head of an executive department are spelled out in considerable detail in the laws passed by Congress, the jobs assigned to these men as a group are not listed in the statutes. The only reference to the Cabinet in the Constitution is a portion of Article 2, which says that the President "may require the opinion, in writing, of the principal officer in each of the executive departments, upon any subject relating to the duties of their respective offices."

Earlier in our history, Cabinet service provided a stepping-stone to the Presidency. Although this is no longer generally true, it is still a high honor to be a federal department head. In addition to commanding one of the highest salaries in the federal government, the Cabinet member enjoys a number of "extras," such as the use of a personal limousine which the government provides. When his Cabinet days are over, a Secretary, which is the official name for the head of an executive department, customarily gets a fitting reminder of his career: the chair that he occupied in the Cabinet Room at the White House is purchased by his fellow Cabinet members and is presented to him.

● *Where the Name Came From*

The term "Cabinet" is not in the Constitution, and was not originally used to describe the President's circle of advisers. As with so

4

many of our institutions, the name came from England. During the seventeenth century, a small group of advisers to King Charles I customarily met in a private room called a cabinet. Slowly — first in derision and later with respect — this word came to be used for the meeting, and then for the group of men themselves.

• *The American and British Systems*

It was natural for the United States to develop the idea of a group of councillors to help the Chief Executive. Before independence, most colonial governments had councils of assistants to advise the governors, and after independence, these groups were provided for by law in many states.

However, the evolution of the American Cabinet was not a conscious imitation of that institution in Great Britain. The forms of government in the two countries are vastly different, both in theory and in practice. Government in the United States is based firmly and basically on the principle of separation of powers: neither the President nor his Cabinet members may hold seats in Congress. Under England's parliamentary system, the prime minister and, usually, every member of his Cabinet are also members of Parliament. They regularly take part in debates and they vote on bills.

The British Cabinet is known collectively as "the government," and the responsibility is collective: The Cabinet as a whole proposes a program, and if Parliament votes against it on an important matter, the Cabinet usually resigns, and a new Parliament is elected. Debate on a proposal is usually led by the Cabinet member whose department is most affected, and most major bills are introduced by Cabinet members.

In the United States, Congress, which includes no member of the executive branch, passes the laws. The President, who has no voice in the legislature, is solely responsible for administering those laws, and the third branch of government — the courts — interprets the laws if and when their legality is questioned.

● Proposals for the American Cabinet

The United States adopted the principle of separation of powers only after other ideas had been proposed and rejected. One proposal called for a council of state to advise the President, consisting of the chief justice of the Supreme Court, the president of the Senate, the speaker of the House of Representatives, and the heads of the executive departments. Another proposal — still suggested by some lawmakers in the twentieth century — would have given seats in Congress to the heads of the executive departments. Although these ideas were dropped, in the earliest days of the republic it did seem that the United States might partly copy the British system just because the executive department heads appeared personally in the halls of Congress. This practice soon ended, however, and today formal appearances in Congress by the executive branch are limited to testimony by Cabinet members and their aides before congressional committees, and to occasional addresses, such as the annual State of the Union speech, by the Chief Executive. While bills are often prepared in the executive branch, they must be introduced, and debate must be conducted, by members of the legislature.

● Beginnings of the American Cabinet

As the Revolutionary War got under way, the Continental Congress wrestled with the problem of creating a new government amidst the strife of conflict. Responsibility for administering military affairs, foreign affairs, finance, and other government functions was entrusted to a group of committees, or boards, usually consisting at least in part of members of Congress. At the end of the war, under the loose form of federal government provided by the Articles of

7

Confederation, the new nation moved toward the present system of concentrating executive responsibility in single heads of departments. The first such jobs created were for the Secretary of Foreign Affairs, the Superintendent of Finance, the Secretary of War, and the Secretary of Marine.

8

- *The First Cabinet under the Constitution*

When the Constitution was ratified in 1789, Congress moved quickly to create the first three departments of government — Foreign Affairs, Treasury, and War. Later that same year, certain domestic responsibilities were added to the duties of the Department of Foreign Affairs, and its name was changed to the Department of State. Although John Jay of New York held the job briefly on an interim basis, Thomas Jefferson of Virginia was the first man appointed as Secretary of State. Alexander Hamilton of New York

9

became the first Secretary of the Treasury, and Henry Knox of Massachusetts became the first Secretary of War. The three departments, headed by these men, became the first Cabinet.

In 1789, Congress also created the office of Attorney General, and the job went to Edmund Randolph of Virginia. Although the Attorney General sat with the three executive department heads from the time the Cabinet was created, he did not become a department head, and thus a full-fledged Cabinet member, until the next century.

The first Cabinet was consulted routinely not only on matters of government policy, but also on purely legal questions. (Originally some had felt that the Supreme Court should render this service, but it was soon decided that the court would give decisions only in actual lawsuits, and would not provide advisory opinions.) The first President of the United States, George Washington (1789-97), was troubled about a controversial bill to create the Bank of the United States. First he asked his Attorney General if the bill was constitutional. Randolph said that it was not. Next the President consulted his Secretary of State, Jefferson, who was of the same opinion. Finally Washington put the question to Hamilton, Secretary of the Treasury. Hamilton felt that Congress had the power to enact the bill. Washington — who apparently never sought the opinion of the other Cabinet member, Secretary of War Knox — sided with Hamilton, the member whose department was most directly involved, and he signed the bank bill into law.

In this first important intra-Cabinet clash of viewpoints, the Secretaries were merely performing their duties, under the Constitution, of rendering "the opinion, in writing" requested by the President. The next step was the regular face-to-face meeting of the Chief Executive with his Cabinet. The first time that the department heads were called together, Washington was not even present. Vice-President John Adams presided in his absence. (It was not until the twentieth century that the Vice-President regularly attended Cabinet meetings.)

During the next few administrations, the practice of taking votes among the Cabinet members on questions of governmental policy started to grow. Sometimes a President would abide by the vote of the majority of his Cabinet. But it was clear from the first that final responsibility was the President's alone.

The President of the United States simply is not allowed to "pass the buck" on executive decisions to his Cabinet members, or to anyone else. As President Harry S Truman (1945-53) said, pointing to his desk: "The buck stops here."

President Abraham Lincoln (1861-65) expressed this principle in another way. The story goes that he put a question to his Cabinet, which then consisted of seven members. All were opposed to the course of action proposed by the President. Lincoln is said to have announced the result of the vote in this manner: "Seven noes, one aye — the ayes have it!"

GROWTH OF THE CABINET

UNDER THE English system, the number of members of the Cabinet is flexible, and it increases and decreases with the needs of the times and the ideas of the prime minister. In the United States, the true Cabinet consists only of the heads of the executive departments, and these must be created by Congress. The trend has been steadily upward, from the original three departments to the present twelve. There has also been an occasional backslide, as when the old War and Navy Departments were merged into a single Department of Defense in 1947. Several of the present departments — such as Agriculture and Interior — originated as minor agencies of other departments. Some — such as Transportation — were created by the transfer of agencies and functions from several departments and independent agencies. Some independent agencies, never parts of established ex-

ecutive departments, were given full-fledged departmental status: for instance, the creation of the Department of Health, Education, and Welfare from the Federal Security Agency.

The rate of change and expansion in the Cabinet has been slow. Most new departments have been created only after years of patient agitation by groups of people who were especially interested in the functions that such departments would perform. The Departments of Labor and Agriculture are examples of this.

13

• How Cabinet Members Are Chosen

Special-interest groups have played an important role not only in the creation of departments but also in the selection of their head men. For example, it is traditional that no Secretary of Labor will be appointed who is not acceptable to major trade-union organizations, and organized groups of farmers are asked for advice in choosing a Secretary of Agriculture.

Some Cabinet members are old friends or even relatives of a President. Others have been chosen without having met the President.

Although Cabinet members are selected by the President, this can be done only "with the advice and consent of the Senate." In almost every case, the President's choice of his Cabinet members has been approved, but there have been a few rejected nominations.

Generally speaking, a President chooses his Cabinet members from his own political party, but there have been frequent exceptions to this rule. President Washington — before the days of party politics — stated the principle that a President could not govern well without having advisers whose ideas were largely in line with his own.

A sort of "coalition" Cabinet — roughly similar to those formed in parliamentary countries when no one party has a majority in parliament — was formed under President John Quincy Adams (1825-29) after the 1824 election had split the Federalist party into factions. It was not long afterward that the idea became firmly established that heads of the executive departments should change with a change of Presidents. So the custom developed of having Cabinet members submit their resignations as a matter of course as soon as a new Chief Executive takes office.

At first, it was felt that this turnover would not be necessary in the case of an "accidental" President — the man who succeeds to the job if the elected President dies in office. President Calvin Coolidge

14

(1923-29), for example, felt obligated to retain the appointees of President Warren G. Harding (1921-23). On the other hand, President Harry S. Truman felt no compulsion to retain the appointees of President Franklin D. Roosevelt. Truman felt that he had the right to choose his own advisers.

At one time it was argued that the consent of the Senate was required to remove a Cabinet member, as well as to appoint him. But soon it became accepted that a President may (although he has rarely had to) fire a Cabinet member on his own.

In the past, Congress was a frequent source of Cabinet members. President Andrew Jackson (1829-37) perhaps set a high mark in this regard. With six Cabinet positions to fill, he chose three members of the Senate and one member of the House of Representatives. But this practice has largely died out. The appointment of Representative Stewart L. Udall of Arizona as Secretary of the Interior by President John F. Kennedy (1961-63) is the only recent example.

● *Geography as a Factor*

The first "Cabinet" — although not then known as such — was too small and the country was too new for geography to have much influence on the selection of members. It was natural that two of Washington's top four advisers should be Virginians, as he was, and that the other two should come from the large states of New York and Massachusetts. Not until James Monroe's Presidency (1817-25) was a deliberate effort made to distribute Cabinet jobs as equally as was reasonably possible among the geographical areas of the nation. Since then, as the country expanded to the Pacific Ocean and as Cabinet posts grew in number, the geographical principle has become rather firmly established. Similar in some respects to the effort to

satisfy special-interest groups with Cabinet appointments, the geographical principle has produced an informal rule: the Secretary of the Interior should be from the Far West, where conservation is considered particularly important; the Secretary of Agriculture should come from the Midwest; the Secretary of Labor should come from a highly industrialized state; and at least one member should be from the President's home state. Democratic Presidents also usually have at least one Southern member in the Cabinet.

These principles were observed, for example, in Lyndon B. Johnson's (1963-   ) Cabinet near the end of his first full term: four Secretaries were from the Northeast, three were from the South, three were from the Midwest, and two were from the West.

16

Since the selection of a Cabinet is, in the final analysis, a matter of intense personal importance to a President, it is natural that Presidents should differ on what they consider most important in choosing these officials. Most Presidents have felt the prime consideration to be personal loyalty, a factor which outweighs loyalty to a particular political party. Woodrow Wilson (1913-21) and Herbert Hoover (1929-33), in particular, felt that personal integrity and administrative ability were more important than party considerations.

THE CABINET MEETING

As WE HAVE SEEN, the regular convening of the President and members of the Cabinet has been customary since George Washington's time. The frequency of these meetings, the way they have been conducted, and their importance have varied with the demands of the times and with the particular personalities and desires of the Presidents.

Soon after the Constitution went into effect, President Washington consulted with his Cabinet on the advisability of his taking a tour of the country. Thereafter, he met with his Cabinet from time to time, but he also made a frequent practice of consulting his department heads individually. By the time the second President, John Adams (1797-1801), took office, the practice of Cabinet meetings was well established. Thomas Jefferson (1801-9) did not like

the idea of having a Cabinet meeting as regularly as once a week. He preferred individual consultations with Cabinet members because it prevented disagreeable collisions. During Andrew Jackson's Presidency, the practice of holding regular Cabinet sessions was largely suspended. Jackson preferred to look for advice from an informal group of friends who came to be known as "the kitchen cabinet." The same was true of President John Tyler (1841-45).

19

But since the time of President James Polk (1845-49), tradition has called for Cabinet meetings to be held at regularly stated intervals. Abraham Lincoln and Woodrow Wilson both wanted to break this tradition and to hold meetings only when they desired, but ultimately they returned to the regular practice. Tuesdays and Fridays came to be known as Cabinet meeting days, although Wilson and other Presidents often cut meetings down to once a week. Under President Lyndon Johnson, the full Cabinet has usually convened every other week.

• Who Attends

The twentieth century has produced the Cabinet meeting which regularly includes nonmembers of the Cabinet. In keeping with the newly enhanced importance of the Vice-Presidency, several recent Presidents have had the Vice-President sit in on meetings. Other officials, such as the ambassador to the United Nations, the budget director, and the heads of certain other non-Cabinet-level agencies, are frequent attenders.

• How a Cabinet Meeting Is Conducted

The Cabinet meets in the Cabinet Room, in the West Wing of the White House. The members sit in black leather armchairs around a large table. Each chair has the name of the Cabinet member on the back of it. Usually the President will open the discussion, seeking advice from each member on problems on the agenda. The loose, informal air of the past disappeared to some extent during the terms of President Dwight D. Eisenhower (1953-61). Deeply imbued

with the concept of staff work learned during his Army career, Eisenhower initiated the idea of having a Cabinet secretary, and his own staff, to prepare an agenda for the meeting, and to take extensive notes. Often a department head gave a fairly elaborate presentation, with the aid of the Cabinet staff, and there were efforts to follow up decisions made at a meeting — something which the Cabinet had notably failed to do in the past. The Cabinet staff idea, and the prepared agenda, were retained after the end of the Eisenhower terms, although without the same degree of formality.

HOW IMPORTANT IS THE CABINET?

THE IMPORTANCE OF the Cabinet meetings and the amount they have accomplished have, of course, varied with the personalities involved. While Presidents Harding and Coolidge perhaps preferred intra-Cabinet harmony above all else, President Truman thought that a lively exchange of differing viewpoints was a most healthy thing.

Some Presidents have leaned heavily on the advice of their Cabinets; others have virtually ignored theirs. Some have wanted each Cabinet member's advice on every major policy decision; others have preferred to get the views of one or more individual members.

President Warren G. Harding leaned very heavily on his Cabinet for help in making decisions. Other Presidents kept the Cabinet in

23

a purely advisory capacity. President Grover Cleveland (1885-89, 1893-97) personally made the decision on just about every important question during his tenure. Some Presidents went so far as to play a leading personal role in the business that was normally conducted by one or more of their Cabinet members. For example, it was often said of Presidents Woodrow Wilson and Franklin D. Roosevelt (1933-45) that each served as his own Secretary of State.

During the terms of the first few Presidents of the United States, the Cabinet consisted of a very small group of men occupying the pinnacle of a very small government bureaucracy. Today, each Cabinet member has a vast domain of his own to control. Just doing his job as a department head is a full-time occupation, leaving him relatively little time in which to do the "homework" necessary to properly fill his second role as a presidential adviser. Since the modern Cabinet has more members than in our early history, a weekly or semiweekly meeting, at which each member has his say on each major issue, would be a most time-consuming affair. The more specialized a particular problem, the more sensible it seems to resolve it by a conference between the President and a single department head, or perhaps two or three. For example, when a serious foreign policy issue is considered, it often makes sense to discuss it only with the Secretaries of Defense and of State, rather than to talk it over at a meeting of the full Cabinet. Similarly, a domestic economic problem might best be discussed with only the Secretaries of Commerce and of Labor.

It seems evident that the Cabinet has decreased significantly in importance during the twentieth century. One aspect of this development has been the creation of a number of important agencies which are completely outside of any of the regular executive departments of the government — for example, the Interstate Commerce Commission, the Federal Trade Commission, and the Atomic Energy Commission.

Other less-specialized groups have gained in importance during times of national or international crisis. Examples of these are Woodrow Wilson's "War Cabinet," consisting of some Cabinet and some non-Cabinet officials; Franklin D. Roosevelt's depression-time "National Emergency Council," and the World War II "War Production Board."

Today, the National Security Council must rate as an advisory body that is more important than the Cabinet. It usually meets about twice a month, also in the Cabinet Room. The President serves as chairman of the National Security Council, which also includes the Vice-President, the Secretary of State, the Secretary of Defense, the Director of the Office of Emergency Planning, the Chairman of the Joint Chiefs of Staff, and the Director of the Central Intelligence Agency. Other officials — such as the Secretary of the Treasury and the Director of the United States Information Agency — are invited to attend from time to time.

Other "extra-Cabinet" organizations and officials have contributed to the decline in the importance of the Cabinet as an advisory and coordinating agency. These include interdepartmental committees containing representatives from two or more executive departments; the Bureau of the Budget and, in particular, its legislative clearance staff; and the White House staff itself, containing presidential assistants who sometimes are the President's closest advisers.

Partly because of its present size, partly because of the complexity of today's problems, the Cabinet has demonstrated serious weaknesses as a body which is responsible for coordinating the work of various departments, and for making direct contributions to decisions through well-informed, well-organized discussions of policy alternatives.

However, this is not to say that the Cabinet has outlived its usefulness. It still serves a useful advisory function to the President, particularly as a sort of political sounding board which is well equipped to provide guidance on the most likely public reactions to proposed policies.

CABINET MEMBERSHIP AS A STEPPING-STONE

ALTHOUGH IT has not been true in recent years, Cabinet membership used to be considered a good stepping-stone to the Presidency. This was particularly true in the case of the Secretary of State. Indeed, President James Monroe is said to have named John Quincy Adams as Secretary of State for the express purpose of putting Adams in line for the Presidency. Besides Adams and Monroe himself, these Secretaries of State went on to the Chief Executive's job: Thomas Jefferson, James Madison, Martin Van Buren, and James Buchanan. James G. Blaine came close; Secretary of State in 1881, he was an unsuccessful presidential candidate in 1884.

Secretaries of War Ulysses S. Grant and William Howard Taft also became President. Herbert Hoover, once Secretary of Commerce, was the last Cabinet member to go on to the top job.

Actually, every member of the Cabinet is, by virtue of his office, in line for the Presidency, should the required number of tragedies occur. Upon the death of a President, the law gives the office to the Vice-President. But should there be no Vice-President to fill the top job — something that has never happened, although eight Presidents have died in office — then the Presidency would pass to the first survivor in this order of Presidential succession, established in 1947: Speaker of the House of Representatives; President Pro Tempore of the Senate; Secretaries of State, Treasury, and Defense; the Attorney General; the Postmaster General; and the Secretaries of Interior, Agriculture, Commerce, Labor, Health, Education, and Welfare, Housing and Urban Development, and Transportation.

No recent President has come from a Cabinet post, because the realities of modern politics have made elective office as a governor or senator, or high-ranking, distinguished wartime military service, a better stepping-stone. In Monroe's time, the very use of a Cabinet appointment as a move toward the Presidency produced considerable jealousy because several members of the Cabinet had presidential ambitions. Andrew Jackson had a reverse theory: He excluded for consideration as members of his Cabinet all those with presidential ambitions.

So it seems that, barring an overwhelming tragedy that would wipe out a large number of our leaders at once, a Cabinet job holds little hope of leading to the White House. But Cabinet members do regularly move on to fine jobs in business and the professions, as well as to further political successes in the Senate or in governorships.

THE DEPARTMENTS

THESE ARE THE twelve departments that are headed by members of the United States Cabinet:

● *The Department of State*

This oldest executive department of the United States government is responsible for the conduct of relations between the United States and other nations, and between the United States and various international organizations.

"State" was created in 1789, shortly before the creation of the Treasury and War Departments. Its original name was Department of Foreign Affairs, which would more accurately describe its present-

30

day functions. Shortly after its creation, Congress changed its name to Department of State, largely because a number of purely domestic chores were added to its responsibilities. For example, the Patent Office started out as an agency of the State Department, and a few domestic jobs — such as keeping the Great Seal of the United States — are still assigned to State.

The department had its origin in the Committee on Secret Correspondence, created by the Continental Congress in 1775 to maintain relations with other nations as the colonies' break with Great Britain drew closer. Next, diplomatic relations became the responsibility of the Congress' Committee for Foreign Affairs. In 1781, the Department of Foreign Affairs was created. Robert Livingston of New York was the first Secretary of Foreign Affairs, followed by John Jay, also of New York. When the Constitution went into effect in 1789, Jay continued as Secretary, and briefly served in the

31

renamed job of Secretary of State, awaiting the arrival of Thomas Jefferson of Virginia, the first man actually selected for that position.

Jefferson had a staff of eight employees, with three diplomatic missions and sixteen consulates abroad. Today, State has more than fifteen thousand employees stationed in more than eighty foreign countries, plus some seven thousand employees at home.

The department is roughly divided into the foreign service and the home service. Foreign-service officers spend most of their careers abroad, in assignments at American embassies, consulates, and other missions, serving occasional tours of duty at desk jobs in Washington. During the course of his career, a foreign-service officer will serve in several parts of the world, usually learning the language, customs, and history of each place to which he is assigned.

Through its foreign-service officers abroad, the department maintains relations with the heads of government and of the ministries of foreign affairs of countries with which the United States has diplomatic relations. Through the Secretary and other officials in Washington, the department stays in contact with other countries' ambassadors to the United States. Ambassadors also conduct the United States' relations with international organizations such as the United Nations and the North Atlantic (NATO) and Southeast Asia Treaty Organizations (SEATO).

One aim of the foreign service is to provide protection to American citizens and business interests abroad, and to maintain a steady flow of information on other nations back to the United States.

In Washington, the Undersecretary of State is the Secretary's principal assistant and adviser, and serves as acting secretary in the Secretary's absence. There are also a number of deputy undersecretaries, who handle administrative matters, liaison with Defense and other departments, and aspects of political and economic policy. Several assistant secretaries oversee foreign service operations in

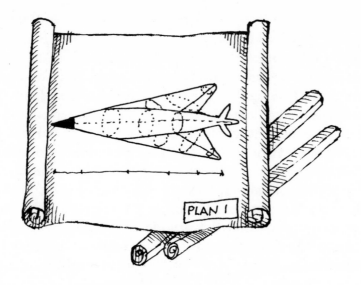

different parts of the world. There is an assistant secretary for Africa, another for Europe, another for Latin America, and so on.

The State Department oversees the issuance of passports to Americans traveling abroad, and the issuance of visas for visits to the United States by persons traveling on foreign passports.

- *The Department of Defense*

The Department of Defense is a single executive department of the government, presided over by a single Cabinet member, which contains within it the Departments of the Army, Navy, and Air Force.

33

In its present form, the department dates from 1949, but the history of the military establishment's representation in the Cabinet goes back to the time of the founding of the nation.

In June, 1776, shortly before adoption of the Declaration of Independence, the Continental Congress created a Board of War and Ordnance. This committee, and a similar one called the Marine Committee, which handled naval affairs, supervised the military operations of the nation until 1781. At that time Congress put the major affairs of government under single executive heads, and resolved that there should be a Superintendent of Finance, a Secretary of War, and a Secretary of Marine.

After adoption of the Constitution in 1789, the second department created by Congress was the Department of War. The first Secretary of War, Henry Knox of Massachusetts, became the second member of President Washington's Cabinet.

The War Department then had naval affairs, as well as operations of the army, under its control. But in 1798, when troubles with England and France gave renewed importance to naval warfare, Congress created a separate Department of the Navy. Its first Secretary was Benjamin Stoddert of Maryland.

This division of responsibility between the War and Navy Departments continued until after World War II. As air power came into prominence, there was a movement for the creation of a separate air force, independent of the army. The Army Air Forces had become virtually an independent branch of the armed forces during World War II, but they remained under the War Department until the National Security Act of 1947. This act created what was called the National Military Establishment, presided over by the first Secretary of Defense, James Forrestal of New York. Under the Secretary, as part of the Military Establishment, were the renamed Department of the Army, the Department of the Navy, and the new Department of the Air Force. Each was considered an executive department of the government, but the individual Secretaries were not considered members of the President's Cabinet. The unification program moved closer to completion in 1949, when the National Military Establishment became known as the Department of Defense. The separate Army, Navy, and Air Force agencies — curiously still called "departments" — became subdivisions of the Department of Defense, and were no longer executive departments of the government in their own right.

Besides the Departments of the Army, Navy, and Air Force, the Department of Defense includes the Joint Chiefs of Staff, consisting of the chairman, the nation's top military officer, and the heads of the Army, Navy, Air Force, and Marine Corps. It also includes a number of agencies which perform centralized services for all the military services — such as the Defense Intelligence Agency, the Defense Communications Agency, and the Defense Supply Agency.

While units of one of the armed services are always responsible to their own service Secretary, through that service's own chain of command, the present unified military organization also includes a number of joint commands. The joint commander of such an organization operates under the direct supervision of the Joint Chiefs of Staff, and is the boss of all units in his command, regardless of which service they belong to.

The best-known function of the Secretary of Defense is the supervision of United States military men, but he also supervises many thousands of civilian employees in his department. He is in charge of the design and procurement of ships, planes, guns, and all sorts of military supplies from private industry. Because this is such an important part of his job, the position of Secretary of Defense has often gone to a prominent industrial leader with great experience in production.

● *The Department of the Treasury*

The third of the departments of government set up immediately after the Constitution went into effect is the Department of the Treasury. The history of the department goes back to the First Continental Congress of 1775 which, faced with the tremendous problem of financing the rapidly approaching struggle for independence, named three men to superintend the printing of two million dollars in bills. A few months later, the Second Continental Congress appointed Michael Hillegas and George Clymer as Joint Treasurers of the United Colonies. Next, a Treasury Committee was appointed by Congress to supervise the efforts of these men. When Clymer resigned to become a member of Congress, Hillegas continued as the single Treasurer for the rest of the Revolutionary War and for the rest of the pre-Constitution period.

A reorganization in 1779 resulted in the creation, for the first time, of the office of Secretary of the Treasury, filled by Robert Troup. However, his office was soon abolished and replaced by a five-member Treasury Board. The Treasury Department was created in 1789, with a single operating head, and the brilliant Alexander Hamilton of New York became the first Secretary of the Treasury under the Constitution.

Hamilton immediately set to work to establish a sound banking system, a stable currency, centralization of government purchasing, and organization of the collection of customs duties, for many years the chief source of government income. One of the first acts that Hamilton obtained from Congress was the creation of a Revenue Marine, the forerunner of the Coast Guard. This service remained a part of the Treasury Department in peacetime until it was transferred to the new Department of Transportation in 1967.

A vast number of nonfiscal responsibilities were first imposed on the Treasury Department. For example, Treasury supervised the postal service until the Post Office Department was created in 1829. Business-related activities were under Treasury control until the Department of Commerce and Labor was created in 1903. (Commerce and Labor became separate departments in 1913.)

Today the main agencies of the Treasury Department are:

The *Internal Revenue Service,* responsible for the collection of federal income, tobacco, and alcohol taxes, and a number of special excise taxes.

The *Secret Service,* whose main responsibilities are detecting and arresting persons who counterfeit, forge, or alter United States currency, coin, and securities, and the protection of the President, Vice-President, and their families. Until formation of the Federal Bureau of Investigation in 1908, the Secret Service was the principal law enforcement agency of the federal government.

The *Bureau of the Mint,* which manufactures and distributes domestic coins, acquires and safeguards the government's stocks of silver and gold, makes coins for certain foreign governments, and produces medals for the armed forces and others.

The *Bureau of Engraving and Printing,* which designs and produces paper money, bonds, and postage and revenue stamps.

The *Bureau of Customs*, which inspects vessels, aircraft, and vehicles in international trade, supervises the collection of import and export duties and certain other taxes, apprehends smugglers, and controls the importation and exportation of certain strategic or contraband materials.

The *Bureau of Narcotics*, which controls the manufacture of certain narcotic drugs, and enforces the laws against the illicit narcotics trade.

The *Bureau of the Public Debt*, which handles the issuance and retirement of bonds and other government securities and generally administers the government's borrowing activities.

The *Office of the Comptroller of the Currency*, responsible for the chartering and supervising of the national banking system.

The *United States Savings Bonds Division*, which promotes the sale of savings bonds and stamps.

The *Office of the Treasurer of the United States*, the official custodian of most of the public funds of the federal government; the Treasurer's signature appears, with that of the Secretary of the Treasury, on our paper money.

- *The Department of Justice*

An act passed in September, 1789, very shortly after the adoption of the Constitution, created the first federal courts and also the job of Attorney General of the United States. The first man named to this position was Edmund Randolph of Virginia.

From early in the administration of George Washington, the Attorney General occupied an important role as an adviser to the President, and he soon was regularly attending Cabinet meetings.

But it was not until 1853 that the Attorney General's salary was equalized with those of Secretaries of the regular executive departments. And it was not until 1870 that the Department of Justice was created, and the Attorney General became a full-fledged Cabinet member ranking with the other department heads.

The 1870 act created the office of Solicitor General, one of the Attorney General's top assistants. The Solicitor General's job includes representing the federal government in many of its cases before the Supreme Court, and generally supervising the government's conduct of cases appealed from the trial courts.

The 1870 act also gave the Attorney General supervision over the United States attorneys, one appointed for each federal judicial district. They prosecute and defend legal proceedings in which the government is interested. The Attorney General also supervises the

United States marshals, who serve papers, guard and transport prisoners, and perform various other functions for the United States District Courts.

The Attorney General has in his department the *Federal Bureau of Investigation*, the famous law enforcement agency created in 1908. The FBI has assumed a steadily increasing role in crime prevention and detection as Congress classifies additional acts as federal crimes.

The Attorney General has control over the *Federal Bureau of Prisons*, which supervises reformatories and penitentiaries for federal prisoners.

The *Immigration and Naturalization Service* is a part of the Department of Justice. It examines aliens coming into this country, to determine if they are legally entitled to admission; it apprehends and deports aliens who have violated the immigration laws; and it registers aliens, and examines persons who wish to apply for United States citizenship.

The purely legal work of the Department of Justice is divided into several divisions, each headed by an assistant attorney general.

The *Criminal Division* assists the local United States attorneys in the enforcement of federal laws. It handles prosecutions ranging from violations of the Migratory Bird Act to the activities of organized racketeers, from interstate transportation of stolen automobiles to kidnapping.

The *Internal Security Division* enforces laws pertaining to the nation's security, such as those dealing with treason, sabotage, registration of foreign agents, and atomic energy.

The *Civil Rights Division* enforces laws guaranteeing freedom to vote and forbidding illegal denial of the rights of citizens, and also enforces laws relating to illegal election practices.

The *Antitrust Division* investigates complaints about violations of antimonopoly laws and other interferences with the freedom of business competition; and, when warranted, institutes the extremely complicated criminal or civil legal proceedings needed to enforce these laws.

The *Tax Division* provides legal assistance to the Internal Revenue Service of the Treasury Department, and to other agencies of the federal government that have problems involving federal, state, or local taxes. It also handles or assists in the handling of lawsuits involving the federal tax laws.

The *Lands Division* handles the acquisition of real estate by the federal government, and also is responsible for litigation affecting the Indian tribes.

The *Civil Division* has general responsibility for noncriminal lawsuits involving the government and not assigned to one of the more specialized divisions of the department.

The *Office of Alien Property* supervises the custody and disposition of property of alien enemies seized by the United States, and also supervises payment of claims against former owners of such property.

● *The Post Office Department*

In addition to the job of delivering the mail at home, and forwarding and receiving mail to and from foreign countries, the Post Office Department sees that subversive or obscene matter is not sent through the mails, negotiates postal treaties with other countries, chooses the design of commemorative and other stamps, and sells money orders.

Efforts to establish a postal system in America began with services set up by the various colonies. Later, the king of England granted a postal monopoly to a private operator. Then Benjamin Franklin of Pennsylvania became one of two joint postmasters general for all of

the colonies, serving until he was dismissed because he sympathized with the colonists' cause in the disputes that led to the Revolutionary War.

In 1775, shortly before the split with Great Britain, Franklin was appointed by the Continental Congress as Postmaster General, and he is generally credited with establishing the basis for a sound, reliable postal system.

After adoption of the Constitution, the office of Postmaster General was set up in the Treasury Department, and Samuel Osgood of Massachusetts was named to the job. The Post Office Department was established by law in 1792, but the Postmaster General did not become a Cabinet officer until 1829, when President Andrew Jackson appointed William T. Barry of Kentucky.

The Post Office Department has the largest number of employees of any department in the federal government, except for the Department of Defense. Usually the Postmaster General has been a man chosen for his political influence rather than an official experienced in postal work. Historically, the Postmaster General has been one of the President's major political advisers. This was logical, for until comparatively recent times, the distribution of postmasterships and other jobs in the postal service was based on political patronage.

● *The Department of the Interior*

Shortly after adoption of the Constitution, some members of Congress suggested the creation of a Home Department to handle purely internal affairs for the new nation. However, others felt that such a move was unnecessary, since many domestic duties could be, and were, assigned to other departments. By 1849, the Departments of State, Treasury, War, and Navy felt that the burden of these internal chores, unrelated to their main responsibilities, had grown too great. A new department was needed to handle them. Thus the Department of the Interior was established in 1849, and Thomas Ewing of Ohio became the first Secretary of the Interior.

The new department was given charge of the Patent Office and the Census Bureau, formerly part of the State Department; the Land Office, formerly under the Treasury; Indian Affairs, formerly part of the War Department's responsibility; and the Pension Bureau, formerly handled by both War and Navy; plus many other functions.

43

For a while, Interior was a sort of general housekeeper for the federal government. However, as more executive departments and independent agencies were created, the department became custodian of the nation's natural resources. Indeed, it has been said that "Department of Natural Resources" would now be a more fitting name for this agency.

Among its other responsibilities, the Department of Interior is responsible for the welfare of some 350,000 members of American Indian tribes, and for the administration of the few American possessions outside the United States — Guam, American Samoas, the Virgin Islands, and the Trust Territory of the Pacific. Its *Bureau of*

Land Management, which over the years has transferred more than one billion acres of land from federal ownership to aid in the country's development, still supervises administration of land and mineral resources on about eight hundred million acres of public lands.

The *National Park Service* operates some two hundred national parks and historic and recreational areas. The *Bureau of Outdoor Recreation* plans an overall national recreational program, including studies of the needs for additional facilities and assistance to states in carrying out their own park and recreational programs.

The *Fish and Wildlife Service* protects and promotes sporting activity for outdoorsmen, and also protects and expands the nation's commercial fishing industry.

The *Bureau of Mines* enforces safety regulations in mines, and engages in research to promote the welfare of the mineral industries. The *Geological Survey* engages in surveys of the topography, mineral and water resources, and geology of the lands of the United States. It also enforces oil, gas, and mining leases, permits, and licenses.

Another important function of Interior is water and power development. This includes the operation of some three hundred dams and reservoirs, and the operation of three power administrations which transmit electricity to several parts of the country.

• *The Department of Agriculture*

Oddly enough, the United States Department of Agriculture, generally referred to as USDA, grew out of the Patent Office, which started as part of the State Department in 1790. Among its other activities, the Patent Office began the distribution of seeds and of agricultural statistics.

The Department of Agriculture was created in 1862, headed by Isaac Newton of Pennsylvania as the first commissioner. It was not until 1889 that the department was raised to Cabinet rank, and was headed by a Secretary. The first Secretary of Agriculture was Norman J. Colman of Missouri.

The work of the USDA changed with advances in scientific knowledge, and with changes in the needs of the American farmer. The work of conserving and reclaiming worn-out farmlands as well as the need to give the farmer a better education, became an early concern of the department. This movement resulted in the far-flung program of the federal-state agricultural extension service, with county agricultural agents in every county, and agricultural experiment stations strategically located throughout the land, working in cooperation with the state agricultural colleges.

Much of the work of the USDA centers around prevention of disease, and ensuring the wholesomeness of food products. USDA inspectors are constantly at work in meat-packing houses, vegetable-producing areas, and wholesale houses, checking products for cleanliness and quality. USDA agents board ships that come in from foreign lands, carefully inspecting them and their cargoes for a variety of insect pests. Researchers are constantly at work developing new forms of farm machinery and ways of using this machinery productively, as well as new ways of marketing farm products.

Providing accurate market data from the agricultural marketing centers of the nation, and from other countries, plays an important part in helping farmers know what to produce and when to sell it.

Through crop insurance and price support programs, the department helps to protect the American farmer against the problems of crop failure and overproduction. America's usually bounteous surplus of foods is put to work at home and abroad through the school milk program, which provides thousands of schools with free or low-cost milk; through the food stamp plan, which helps low-income families stretch their food dollars; and through the distribution of foods to charitable institutions at home and to the hungry in other lands, often with the cooperation of private relief agencies.

The USDA also has a variety of programs to make credit available to the farmer, who is faced with the need for an increasingly heavy investment in land and equipment to keep pace with the technological advances in agriculture.

Another important activity of the department is the *Agricultural Rural Electrification Administration*. This service provides electricity through rural cooperatives, and has brought laborsaving electrical energy to about 97 per cent of America's farm families, compared to about 11 per cent in the 1930's. Telephone service is also provided by some of these cooperatives.

● *The Department of Commerce*

The Department of Commerce is the business agency of the federal government, generally charged with the job of promoting the foreign and domestic commerce of the nation.

Like other government departments, its activities have changed and expanded with the times. Its work includes one of the oldest activities of the federal government — taking the census, which has been required every ten years since 1790; and one of the newest — urging foreigners to travel in the United States. It includes the Patent Office, and the nation's newest and oldest governmental scientific research organizations.

In 1903, the Department of Commerce and Labor was established, with George B. Cortelyou of New York as the first Secretary. Ten years later, labor activities were split off into a new and separate Department of Labor, and the present Department of Commerce was created, with William C. Redfield of New York as Secretary.

Until the Department of Transportation was created in 1967, a major part of the activities of the Department of Commerce was in the transportation field, including federal aid to highways under its Bureau of Public Roads.

Today, the Secretary of Commerce supervises in four main areas, each headed by an assistant secretary:

The assistant secretary for *Science and Technology* has charge of the *Environmental Sciences Services Administration*, which includes

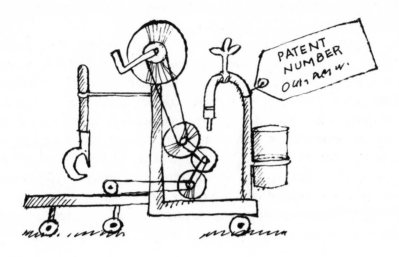

the *Weather Bureau*, the *Coast and Geodetic Survey*, and several other scientific agencies. This area of Commerce also controls the *National Bureau of Standards*, which provides the central basis for our system of measurements, and assists industry by supplying scientific data on materials. The *Patent Office*, which protects the rights of inventors, is also under Science and Technology.

The assistant secretary for *Economic Affairs* supervises the *Bureau of the Census* which, in addition to counting heads every ten years, is constantly conducting surveys and turning out statistical reports on housing, manufacturing, local government, retail trade, and other matters. Economic Affairs also controls the *Office of Business Economics*, which analyzes and reports on national income, the balance of international payments, and other aspects of the national economy.

The assistant secretary for *Domestic and International Business* supervises, among other things, the *Business and Defense Services Administration*, which deals with the national industrial mobilization program. This section of Commerce also stimulates modernization of American industry, and generally promotes cooperation between business and government to promote greater productivity, employment, and profits. It has charge of the *Bureau of International Commerce*, which helps American businessmen market their goods abroad, the latter including among its functions negotiations with foreign governments, supplying United States businessmen with information on business conditions abroad, and promoting trade fairs and trade missions.

The assistant secretary for *Economic Development* has charge of the *Economic Development Administration*, which assists local efforts at creating new industry and steady employment in areas where they are most needed. Economic Development also supervises public-works programs, business loans, technical assistance, and research and planning, as well as the *Office of Regional Economic Development*, which coordinates the work of regional commissions in preparing economic development plans.

● *The Department of Labor*

A long campaign by workingmen's organizations to have a Cabinet-level department for the welfare of wage earners resulted in a separate Department of Labor in 1913.

The present department originated as a bureau within the Department of Interior in 1884. Four years later a Department of Labor was established, but its head did not have Cabinet status. In 1903, legislation created the Department of Labor and Commerce. Finally, on March 4, 1913, President William Howard Taft (1909-13) signed a bill creating a new Department of Labor, headed by a Secretary who was a member of the President's Cabinet. The first Secretary was William B. Wilson of Pennsylvania. The first woman to hold a Cabinet post was a Secretary of Labor: Frances Perkins, appointed by President Franklin D. Roosevelt.

The work of this department has varied with the times, but compiling statistics has always been an important function. The Labor Department administered the laws governing immigration and the naturalization of aliens until that duty was transferred to the Justice Department. It supervised the bureau concerned primarily with protection of children until some of those functions were given to the Department of Health, Education, and Welfare. The Department of Labor administers the steadily growing body of laws that deal with labor relations, wages and hours, and working conditions. In the economic depression of the 1930's the department found work for the needy and job training for the unemployed, and it created new jobs through public works. Wartime switched that emphasis to mobilization of the nation's manpower for greater production.

● *The Department of Health, Education, and Welfare*

The Federal Security Agency, an independent body, was transformed into the Department of Health, Education, and Welfare on April 11, 1953. Mrs. Oveta Culp Hobby of Texas, then the Federal Security Administrator and formerly commander of the Women's Army Corps, became the first Secretary of this department.

The Secretary supervises a wide variety of activities; many of them in partnership with state and local governments.

The major units of the department are:

The *Social Security Administration*, which receives taxes from persons covered by the system (nine out of ten working Americans), and provides monthly benefits to retired or disabled members, to their dependents, and to their survivors. This administration also supervises the federal medical care program.

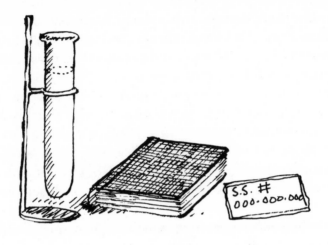

The *Public Health Service*, which originated in 1798 as a part of the Treasury Department to provide medical care for sick and injured seamen. This agency operates a number of hospitals, quarantine stations, and medical research centers. It compiles health statistics, assists states in the control of epidemics and communicable diseases and the sanitation of milk and water supplies, and administers the federal programs for construction of hospitals, research facilities, and sewage treatment works.

The *National Institutes of Health*, created in 1930, is a particularly well-known part of the Public Health Service. The major research unit of the service, it occupies a 305-acre tract in Bethesda, Maryland, where research to combat the major killing and crippling diseases is conducted. Seven institutes are included: those on cancer; mental health; heart disease; arthritis and metabolic diseases; neurological diseases and blindness; allergy and infectious diseases; and dental research. The NIH also handles federal funds granted for research in many nonfederal institutions.

The *Office of Education*, established in 1867, whose functions include research, dissemination of information, and promotion of education throughout the nation. The office provides a variety of services to local and state school officials, and to colleges and other educational organizations. It administers programs of federal financial assistance for a wide variety of educational activities on all levels.

The *Welfare Administration*, which helps finance and supervise the programs of public assistance for the aged, the disabled, and needy children and adults. It also engages in many research and training projects in this field, including programs for combating juvenile delinquency. State and local governments also contribute to public assistance programs.

The *Food and Drug Administration*, an important guardian of the nation's health, which keeps a close watch over the purity and truthful labeling of foods, drugs, and cosmetics. The administration's laboratories test these items, and FDA personnel review manufacturers' evidence of the safety of new products.

The *Vocational Rehabilitation Administration*, another educational agency which cooperates with the states in restoring to useful employment men and women who have job handicaps.

The *Federal Water Pollution Control Administration*, which, like comparable state and local agencies, assists in tackling the increasingly serious problem of spoilage of our rivers and streams by sewage and industrial wastes.

The *Administration on the Aging*, the newest agency of the Department of Health, Education, and Welfare, which works closely with other agencies in providing information and assistance to help solve the special problems of older persons.

● *The Department of Housing and Urban Development*

On September 9, 1965, the special problems of America's growing cities were represented by a Cabinet-level department, when President Johnson signed a bill creating the Department of Housing and Urban Development. Robert C. Weaver of the District of Columbia, then administrator of the Housing and Home Finance Agency, was named as the first Secretary. He was also the first Negro to be named to a Cabinet-level post in the federal government.

As early as 1912, there had been talk of creating a "Department of Municipalities" as a study group, not as a Cabinet-level executive department of the government. Forty-two years later, legislation for creating a new executive department (named by its sponsor "the Department of Urbiculture") was introduced in Congress. Similar bills were offered in later sessions of Congress, all without success until adoption of the 1965 legislation.

Significant legislation in the housing field long preceded the creation of the department. In 1892, Congress appropriated funds to investigate slums in four large American cities. The first direct federal aid in the housing field came during World War I, when money was voted to provide needed housing for defense workers. The next significant action came during the great depression of the 1930's, when the Federal Home Loan Bank Board, the Home Owners' Loan

Corporation, the Federal Housing Administration, the Federal National Mortgage Association, and the Federal Savings and Loan Insurance Corporation were formed. The first federal low-rent housing program followed in 1937, and during and after World War II, programs for war workers and veterans were established. The National Housing Agency was created by executive order in 1942, bringing under a single agency all nonfarm housing programs of the federal government. This agency became the Housing and Home Finance Agency under the reorganization plan of 1947. Other new programs were added to this agency, before it reached Cabinet status, including the slum clearance and redevelopment, community facilities, and college housing plans, and extensions of existing aid-to-housing programs. Federal aid to local transportation systems, later transferred to the Department of Transportation, were first assigned to the Housing and Home Finance Agency and later to the Department of Housing and Urban Development.

56

● *The Department of Transportation*

The newest department of the federal government is the Department of Transportation, which began operations on April 1, 1967, with Alan S. Boyd of Florida as the first Secretary. Its creation demonstrated an awareness of the need for a cohesive national transportation policy, and for the centralized direction of solutions to the transportation problems that involve the nation's growing cities, its passenger railroads, and its vastly increased air travel.

The new department includes:

The *Federal Aviation Agency*, formerly an independent body, whose functions include the operation of air traffic control and navigation systems, federal aid to airports, and certification of aircraft and airmen.

The *Federal Highway Administration*, which includes the *Bureau of Public Roads*, formerly part of the Commerce Department. This administration supervises the interstate highway program, federal aid to state road systems, and the federal highway safety program.

The *United States Coast Guard*, formerly a part of the Treasury Department in peacetime, and still a part of the Navy Department in time of war. The Coast Guard's duties include rescue and law enforcement at sea, certification of seamen and of vessels, investigation of accidents at sea, and operation of navigational aids.

The *Federal Railroad Administration*, which took over operation of the Alaska Railroad from the Interior Department, and which also includes an important research and development agency, the *Office of High-Speed Ground Transportation*.

INDEX